MW00339577

FORENSIC Investigations

BODY TALK

Looking at Biological Evidence

Leela Burnscott

Smart Apple Media

Smart Apple Media
P.O. Box 3263
Mankato, MN 56002

First published in 2009 by
MACMILLAN EDUCATION AUSTRALIA PTY LTD
15–19 Claremont Street, South Yarra 3141

Visit our website at www.macmillan.com.au or go directly to www.macmillanlibrary.com.au

Associated companies and representatives throughout the world.

Copyright © Leela Burnscott 2009

Library of Congress Cataloging-in-Publication Data

Burnscott, Leela.
    Body talk: looking at biological evidence / Leela Burnscott.
       p. cm. — (Forensic investigations)
    Includes index.
    ISBN 978-1-59920-458-1 (hardcover)
    1. Forensic sciences—Juvenile literature. 2. Evidence, Criminal—Juvenile literature. 3. Criminal investigation—Juvenile literature.
    4. Crime scene searches—Juvenile literature. I. Title.
    HV8073.8.B865 2010
    363.25'62—dc22

                                      2009000383

Edited by Georgina Garner
Text and cover design by Cristina Neri, Canary Graphic Design
Page layout by Raul Diche
Photo research by Sarah Johnson
Illustrations by Alan Laver, Shelly Communications

Printed in the United States

Acknowledgments

The author and the publisher are grateful to the following for permission to reproduce copyright material:

Front cover photograph: Forensic blood sample. A forensic scientist delicately removes a fragment of material from a bloodstained garment recovered from a crime scene. The fabric will be used to extract a blood sample for DNA fingerprinting © Dr Jurgen Scriba/ Science Photo Library

Background images used throughout pages: fingerprint courtesy of iStockphoto/James Steidl; tweezers courtesy of iStockphoto/ Mitar Holod; forensic investigation kit courtesy of iStockphoto/Brandon Alms.

Images courtesy of: Simone Crepaldi/AAP Image, **29**; © Department of Defence, **30** (bottom left); Fairfax/Kate Geraghty, **20** (top); Image copyright © Forensic Behavioral Services International, **26** (bottom); Getty Images/Dan Trevan/AFP, **4** ; Getty Images/Robert Sherbow/Time Life Pictures, **26** (top); iStockphoto, **25** (left); iStockphoto/Brad Killer, **27**; iStockphoto/Brandon Alms, **20** (bottom); iStockphoto/Brendan Baeza Stanicic, **22**; iStockphoto/Eliza Snow, **14**; iStockphoto/Joseph Abbott, **11**; From RJ Johansen and CM Bowers, "Digital Analysis of Bitemark Evidence, 2002, published by Forensic Imaging Institute, Santa Barbara, CA", **19**; Photo Researchers/Photolibrary, **16** (all), **17** (bottom); AJ Photo/Science Photo Library/Photolibrary, **24**, **30** (bottom right); Dave Roberts/ Science Photo Library/Photolibrary, **17** (top); James Stevenson/Science Photo Library/Photolibrary, **25** (right); Jim Varney/Science Photo Library/Photolibrary, **30** (middle right); Mauro Fermariello/Science Photo Library/Photolibrary, **12**; Michael Donne, University of Manchester/Science Photo Library/Photolibrary, **15** (all); Pascal Goetgheluck/Science Photo Library/Photolibrary, **30** (top left); Pasquale Sorrentino/Science Photo Library/Photolibrary, **9**; Peter Menzel/Science Photo Library/Photolibrary, **10**; Philippe Psaila/ Science Photo Library/Photolibrary, **5**, **7**; Volker Steger/Science Photo Library/Photolibrary, **8**; Shutterstock/Barbara Quinn, **21**; Shutterstock/Juan David Ferrando Subero, **18**; Shutterstock/Mundoview, **13**; Image copyright © Victorian Institute of Forensic Medicine, **30** (middle left and top right); © Vienna Report Agency/Sygma/Corbis, **28**.

While every care has been taken to trace and acknowledge copyright, the publisher tenders their apologies for any accidental infringement where copyright has proved untraceable. Where the attempt has been unsuccessful, the publisher welcomes information that would redress the situation.

Contents

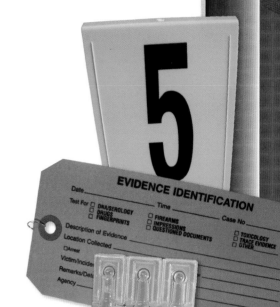

GLOSSARY WORDS

When a word is printed in **bold**, you can look up its meaning in the Glossary on page 31.

Science in the Court!

Forensic science is the use of scientific knowledge and techniques within the legal system, particularly in the investigation of crime. Forensic science can:

- determine if an **incident** resulted from an accident, natural causes, or a criminal act
- identify those involved in the incident
- identify and find those people responsible for the incident
- make sure that the innocent are not wrongly convicted

The term "forensic science" is quite misleading because it suggests only one type of science is involved. This is certainly not the case. Forensic investigations can involve virtually every field of science and technology, from electronics to psychology.

Forensic investigations require the skills of specially trained police, scientists, doctors, engineers, and other professionals. These investigators examine all types of evidence, from bloodstains to weapons and from bugs to computers. The greater the pool of evidence against an accused person, the greater the chance of a conviction.

A forensic expert presents crime scene photographs during a trial.

Body Talk

Without saying a word, both a victim's and an offender's body can tell a forensic investigator a great deal, such as:

- who a victim is
- who injured or killed a victim
- where an incident occurred and when

DNA (deoxyribonucleic acid), blood type, bone structure, and dental patterns are just some of the things that make people different from each other. These are also some of the things that can be examined in forensic investigations.

By studying people's thoughts and behavior, forensic psychologists can also discover many things, such as:

- the type of person that is likely to have committed a crime
- if that person is likely to offend again
- how a person deals with society

Studying the nature of humans has a large role to play in solving cases. This type of forensic science is often called forensic or psychological profiling.

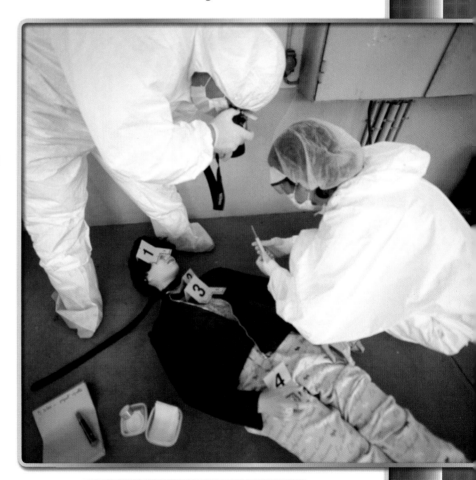

Forensic investigators photograph and examine a murder victim during a training exercise.

DNA

Deoxyribonucleic acid (DNA) is the building block of most living creatures. A person's DNA forms their individual **genetic information**, which is reproduced identically, again and again, in their cells. It is what determines all the characteristics of a person, such as their height, skin color, and health.

Under the Microscope

DNA is made up of four compounds, called bases, which are found in pairs:

- adenine (A) is found with thymine (T)
- guanine (G) is found with cytosine (C)

DNA base pairs are joined together, forming a twisted ladder-like structure called a double helix. Only small sections of the DNA double helix have coded instructions. These sections are called genes and are what shape an individual.

The DNA in a normal human cell is shared between 23 pairs of chromosomes. These chromosomes contain a total of about 25,000 genes.

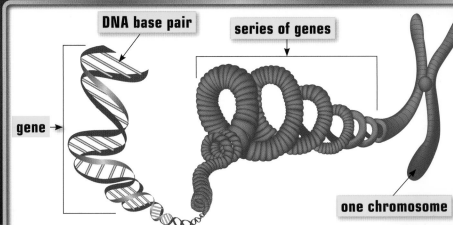

DNA base pair

series of genes

gene

one chromosome

DNA base pairs form a ladder-like structure, called a double helix.

DID YOU KNOW?

American James Watson and Englishman Francis Crick discovered the double helix structure of DNA in 1953.

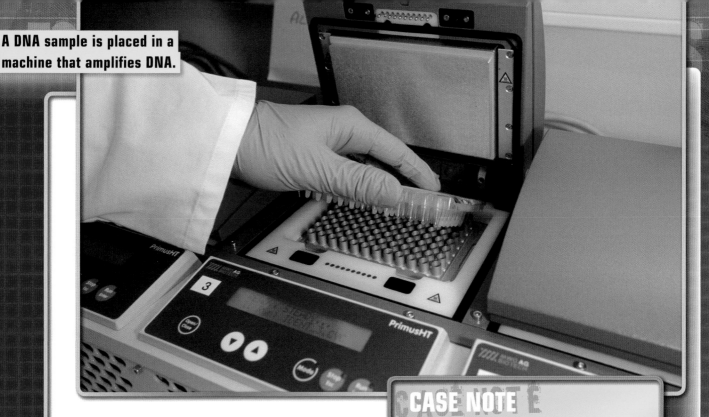

DNA Evidence

DNA can be found in blood, saliva, body tissue, **hair sheaths**, sweat, and other body fluids. DNA does not break down quickly, so it can be recovered from material that is old and decayed. If only small amounts are recovered, the DNA can be amplified, or copied many times, so there is enough to work with.

CASE NOTE

Identical twins have identical DNA. This means forensic investigators need more than just DNA to prove which twin was involved in an incident.

DNA evidence can help answer many questions, including:

• whether unidentified remains are human or animal

• who an unidentified victim is

• who was present at an incident

To answer these questions, scientists work out the order of A–T and C–G base pairs along sections of someone's DNA strand, such as ATCGCGAT. This is called DNA sequencing, typing, or profiling.

If the sequence from the DNA evidence does not match a suspect then the suspect was probably not involved and is excluded. If the DNA sequence matches, then this only indicates that the sample could have come from the suspect. Unlike in television shows and movies, DNA evidence alone never results in a conviction.

DNA Sequencing

DNA sequencing is very useful in forensic investigations, but it is still only a relatively new science and is not always recognized by courts.

The full DNA sequence in a human chromosome has between 50 million to 250 million base pairs. When forensic investigators look at DNA sequences, they look only at very small parts of the full DNA sequence. They look for repetitions in parts of certain genes. If two samples have matching repetitions at these points, it is likely that the two samples came from the same person. If they do not match, the samples could not have come from the same person.

DID YOU KNOW?

Most countries have their own national DNA **database** for storing DNA sequences from crime scenes. To help fight global crimes such as terrorism, the United States, Australia, United Kingdom, Canada and New Zealand authorities are looking at establishing an international DNA database.

A forensic scientist holds a DNA sample in a test tube.

The Process of DNA Sequencing

A common method of amplifying DNA is called polymerase chain reaction (PCR).

First, the DNA is split into small fragments by an **enzyme**, such as a polymerase. A dye is added to a sample of the DNA fragments, which is then loaded onto a slab of special gel. An electric current is run through the gel, causing the fragments to move through it. The smaller fragments move faster than the bigger ones, so the fragments get separated and ordered by size. The dye is used to track the DNA fragments as they move through the gel to see when the first strands reach the bottom.

When finished, a nylon membrane is placed over the gel. This transfers the DNA to the membrane, which is then radioactively labeled. The membrane is placed under X ray film, which produces an exact copy of the DNA sequence when developed. Scientists read the DNA sequence or profile from the X ray film.

CASE NOTE

It is very important that a DNA sample is not contaminated. DNA analysis must be done under strict conditions, and scientists should always wear gloves.

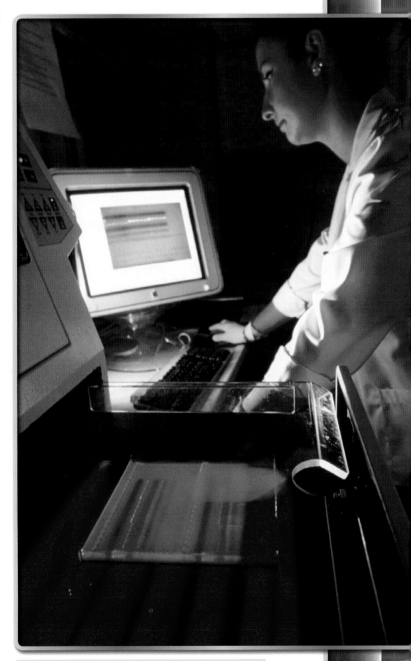

A forensic investigator analyzes a DNA sample that has been sequenced.

Blood

Blood is often an important part of a forensic investigation. Blood evidence may involve:

- blood typing, which is also called blood grouping
- bloodstain and spatter patterns
- blood clotting

Blood typing helps narrow down the identity of a victim, suspect, and anybody else present at a crime scene. Whenever an injury causes bleeding, there will be some dripping, spraying, spattering, or smearing of blood at a scene. Studying these patterns can help work out how, where, and when a person was injured. Checking if blood has clotted can help **forensic pathologists** work out when a person died and if they received their injuries **ante-mortem** or **post-mortem**.

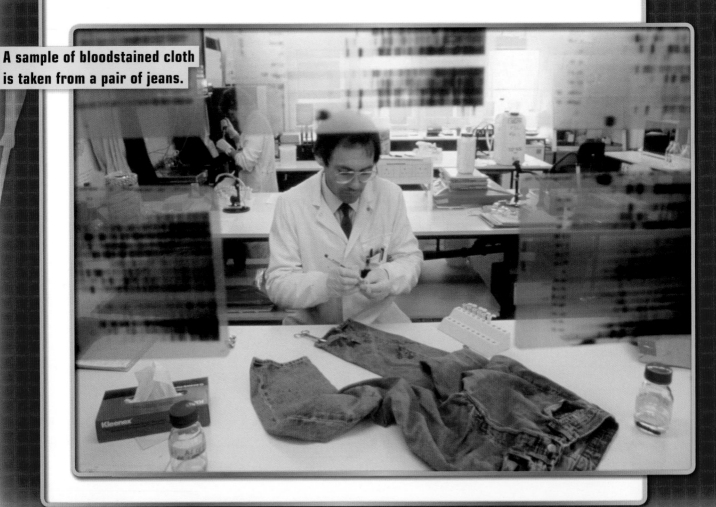

A sample of bloodstained cloth is taken from a pair of jeans.

Blood Typing

Unlike their fingerprints, a person's blood is not unique, so it can never be used for exact identification. Finding out the blood type of the blood evidence, however, can quickly rule out people not involved in an incident or build up the pool of evidence against those who were. Blood cells can be found in saliva and semen, too.

The Process of Blood Typing

A simple and quick test is used to check if a blood sample is human or animal. Human blood is then typed to determine if it is type A, AB, B, or O.

The blood is typed further and is matched to one of at least 288 different blood groups. Because blood degrades very quickly, typing may not always be possible.

Under the Microscope

In 1901 to 1902, Austrian Karl Landsteiner discovered that every human's blood belonged to one of four blood groups: A, AB, B, or O. By 1940, another characteristic of blood, called the Rhesus factor, was discovered. If blood contains Rhesus factor, it is called positive (+). If it does not, it is called negative (-).

The ABO and Rhesus blood grouping systems are still used today. Many other blood factors have also been discovered. Some, like the MN group, are found in some races but not in others.

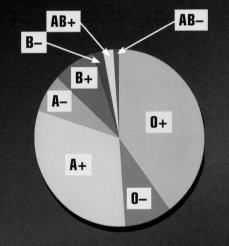
Frequency of ABO blood types in Australia

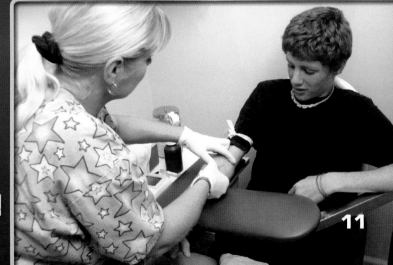
A pathology collector takes blood from a child for typing.

11

Bloody shoeprints are measured and analyzed at a crime scene.

Bloodstain Pattern Analysis

Blood is pumped through blood vessels around the body under high pressure. When a person is stabbed, shot, or hit with great force, the skin and blood vessel will usually break. This allows blood to leak out. When a major blood vessel is broken, blood shoots out, spraying everything in its path.

When a bloody object is swung in the air, some of the blood is flung off. This produces a characteristic pattern called cast off.

Forensic examiners study:

- individual blood drop sizes and shapes
- the location and pattern of blood spray and cast-off blood
- the shape and direction of blood smears

Blood Clotting

When a person bleeds, their body immediately produces **clotting factors** to stop the flow of blood. These factors cause blood to thicken up, flow more slowly, and plug up the "escape route" of the blood. When injuries are very severe, however, natural clotting factors are not enough to stop the flow and people can bleed to death.

When a person dies, they stop producing clotting factors and the blood remains fluid. If blood runs freely when a dead person's bruise is cut, this tells a pathologist that the injury was most likely received after death.

By studying the color of a person's bruise, pathologists can get a rough idea of how long ago an injury occurred. A blue–black bruise is fresh, but a yellow–brown one could be days or even a week old. People bruise and clot at different rates, however, so pathologists know that these are not hard facts.

The colors of a bruise can help pathologists estimate the age of an injury.

Bones

Sometimes, all that remains of a victim are their bones. A forensic anthropologist is normally the first expert called in to examine bones. Anthropologists study the physical development of humans. A zoologist, who studies animals, may be called in to determine if the bones come from animals.

The skull, limb, and pelvic bones are generally the most useful bones to forensic examiners. They can help reveal:

- if the bones are human or animal
- the victim's identity
- the cause of death

Cause of Death

A crushed skull or badly broken limbs suggest that a victim was severely beaten, hit by a vehicle, or fell from a great height. When only small fractures, such as hairline fractures, are present, great force was probably not used. Bones can also be examined for traces of poison and other chemicals.

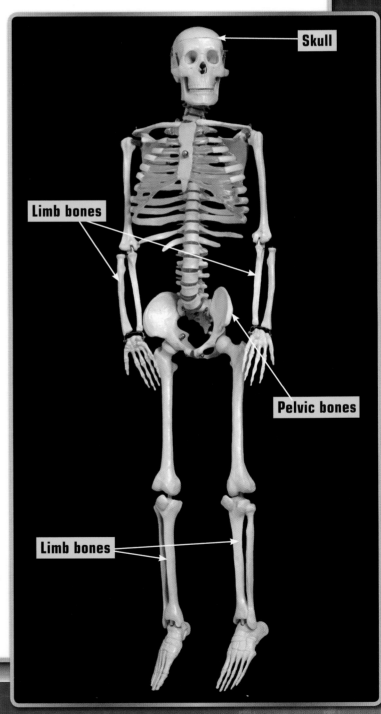

Skull

Limb bones

Pelvic bones

Limb bones

The skull, limb, and pelvic bones are very useful for identification.

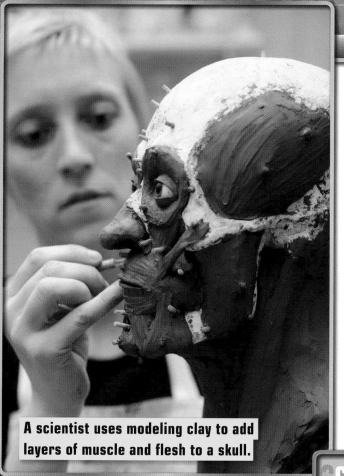

A scientist uses modeling clay to add layers of muscle and flesh to a skull.

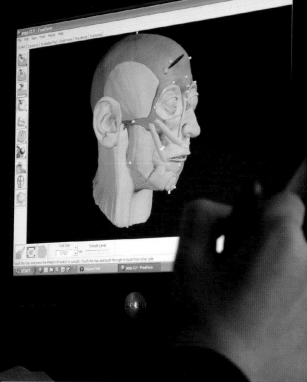

A computer can be used to reconstruct the features of a face using the shape of the skull.

Facial Characteristics

The skull is the most useful bone for victim identification. This is because the shape of the skull, especially the depth of the cheekbones and eye sockets, controls what a person looks like. Muscles and **ligaments** are attached to the skull and take on its shape. In turn, these shape the flesh of the face. If the teeth are still attached to the jawbone, they can also be used to identify the victim.

Around the world, there are highly skilled scientists who can use the skull to reconstruct a person's face. They make a cast of the skull, and then build up layers of muscle and flesh with modeling clay, producing a model of the face.

CASE NOTE

The skull reconstruction technique was probably first used in 1894 by Wilhelm His. Using a cast of a skull thought to belong to the famous composer Johann Sebastian Bach (1685–1750), he reconstructed Bach's face. In 2008, the same cast was used to generate another reconstruction of Bach's face. This time, computer modeling was used. Computer modeling uses layers of digital data, instead of modeling clay, to build up an image.

Other Physical Characteristics

The skull, along with other bones, can reveal many physical characteristics of a victim, such as those that indicate gender, height, and age.

Gender

There are some small differences between the bones of males and females. Some of the differences are that:

- female bones are usually smaller and lighter, and have shallow grooves where the muscles attach
- a female's hips and pelvic bone opening are wider
- male skulls are a slightly different shape, with bigger, more obvious ridges over the eyebrow area

Height

A person's height can be roughly calculated by measuring the length of their limb bones. This is because bone-length proportions in humans are usually the same. The length of the bone from ankle to knee is almost the same as the bone length from knee to hip, no matter how short or tall a person is.

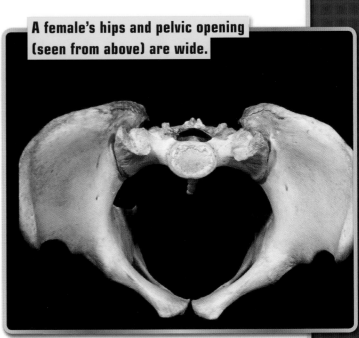
A female's hips and pelvic opening (seen from above) are wide.

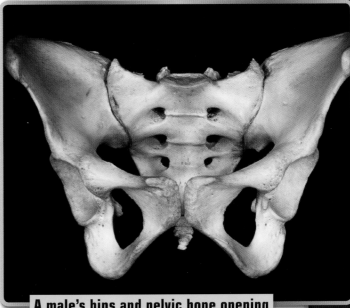
A male's hips and pelvic bone opening (seen from the front) are narrow.

DID YOU KNOW?

The distance from fingertip to fingertip of a person's outstretched arms is almost the same as the height of that person from head to toe.

Age

The probable age of a person can be estimated by the size, weight, and development of their bones. Bones of children are smaller, lighter, and less developed than adult bones. Bones become larger, heavier, and fully formed, and fuse together as a person develops from a teen to an adult. In older adults, bones weaken, become lighter, and break more easily.

More specific estimates of age can be made by looking at whether certain bones have fused and developed fully, because:

- large bone plates of the skull are separate at birth and then fuse at set rates until they fully fuse at 30 years old
- arm bones develop fully in women at around age 18 and in men at age 19
- thighbones stop developing at around ages 18 to 20
- the hipbone is fully fused at age 24
- the collarbone is the last long bone to fuse, at around age 25

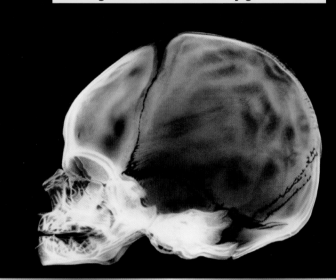

The bone plates in a baby's skull are separate and begin to fuse as the baby grows older.

The bone plates in an adult's skull are fused into one piece of bone.

Teeth

A person's teeth are almost as unique as their fingerprints. A forensic dentist, called a forensic **odontologist**, can estimate a victim's age and even determine their identity by their teeth. Odontologists can also use bite marks to identify a biter.

Key features odontologists look for are:

- shape and size of individual teeth
- wear patterns and damage to teeth
- dental work, such as fillings and braces
- the arrangement and spacing of the teeth in the jawbone

To identify a person, an odontologist compares post-mortem dental records to ante-mortem records. Often, X rays are taken or casts of bite marks are made. Fortunately, many people go to the dentist every two to five years, so they have good ante-mortem dental records.

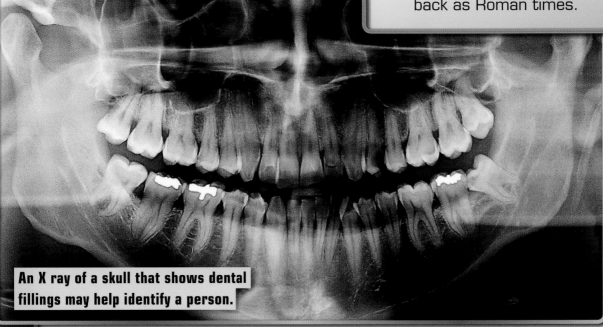

An X ray of a skull that shows dental fillings may help identify a person.

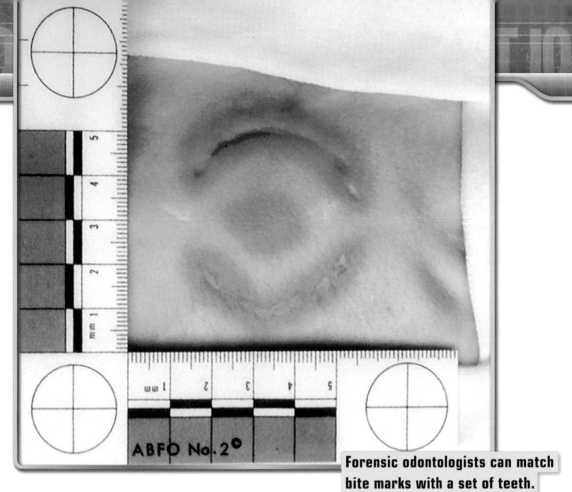

Forensic odontologists can match bite marks with a set of teeth.

Bite Marks

Each person is thought to produce a unique bite mark. This uniqueness is based on the number and shape of teeth, the spacing and arrangement of the teeth, and any damage to the teeth. Forensic odontologists compare bite marks to a person's dental records or to a cast of their teeth.

Age

Teeth, like bones, can help determine a person's age, generally to within one to two years. Teeth develop at a fairly regular rate. The first set of teeth, called baby or primary teeth, start growing at around six months of age and form fully by three years of age. Permanent, or adult, teeth slowly replace these baby teeth from around six years of age.

Some of the key facts about teeth are:

- only about 20 baby teeth are grown, but 32 adult teeth are produced
- the baby molar tooth is bigger than the adult molar tooth
- wisdom teeth are the last to grow, usually starting at ages 17 to 21

Prints

The use of fingerprint identification is over 115 years old. Fingerprints are a universally accepted piece of evidence. New techniques such as hand and footprint identification are starting to prove just as useful, too.

Fingerprints

The skin on each person's fingers carries a unique pattern of ridges and grooves. Investigators use the shape, length, and arrangement of these ridges to identify people.

A fingerprint is a copy of a finger's ridge pattern. It is formed by oil and sweat that is constantly released through **pores** in the skin. Fingerprints can be left on any surface, but the most clear, well-formed ones are left on smooth, damp, or dusty surfaces.

Fingerprints are collected and compared directly to a victim's or suspect's fingerprint, or to fingerprints stored on a database. Most countries have well-established fingerprint databases.

A fingerprint expert uses special lighting to detect fingerprints that are otherwise invisible.

DID YOU KNOW?
Not even identical twins have identical fingerprints.

By dusting surfaces with brightly colored powder, otherwise invisible fingerprints can be recovered from solid surfaces such as door handles.

Footprints and Handprints

The skin on a person's hands and feet is also thought to have unique ridge patterns. Forensic investigators can compare footprints or handprints found at a crime scene to prints of a victim or suspect.

Footprints and handprints are useful forensic tools even if the ridge pattern cannot be determined. The size and shape of these types of prints reflect a person's age, height, and body shape, which can help narrow down who left the prints. A tall, skinny person will produce a much longer and slimmer print than a short, overweight person. A child's print will be much smaller than an adult's print.

It is thought that everyone puts different amounts of force on the different parts of their feet as they walk. This means that people produce uniquely shaped prints, too. When a print is left in soft material such as soil, a cast can be made. This cast can be compared to a suspect's foot or a suspect may be asked to dip their feet in a tray of ink and walk on white paper. These prints may also be compared to photographs of prints found at a crime scene.

CASE NOTE

There are no national databases of footprints or handprints, however, palm and handprints taken from crime scenes are sometimes added to national fingerprint databases.

A person puts different amounts of force or pressure on different parts of their feet when they stand, producing uniquely shaped footprints.

Pathology

One of the goriest jobs in forensic investigations is that of the pathologist. They are the doctors who try to work out the time and cause of someone's death. To do this, they examine a body both externally and internally, and they sometimes even examine the crime scene.

Crime Scene Investigation

At a crime scene, the pathologist takes note of the body's placement and condition, the temperature at the scene, the temperature of the body, the past weather in the area, and any factors that may have contributed to the person's death. The pathologist may also examine any blood spatter found at the scene.

External Examinations

Once the body is at the **mortuary**, the pathologist thoroughly examines the body externally, or from the outside. The pathologist looks for signs of **rigor mortis**, **livor mortis**, wounds, and any identifying marks, such as tattoos or signs of old injuries or operations.

DID YOU KNOW?

Pathologists must investigate all sudden, unexplained, or suspicious deaths. These include deaths in hospitals, nursing homes, private homes, and prisons. Most pathologists only spend a small part of their time looking at victims of violent crime.

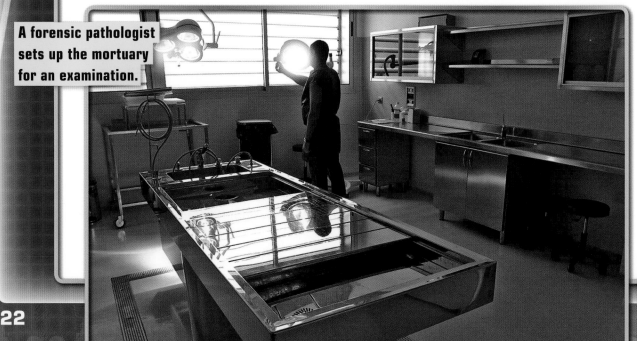

A forensic pathologist sets up the mortuary for an examination.

Rigor Mortis

Rigor mortis is the stiffening of the body after death. This stiffening usually begins three hours after death and lasts about 36 to 48 hours. By looking for signs of rigor mortis, the pathologist can estimate the time of death.

Livor Mortis

When a person dies, their blood pools at the body's lowest points in a process called livor mortis. This produces bruise-like patches in these areas, called lividity. Livor mortis does not occur in areas under pressure, such as the part of an arm on which the head is resting. The skin in these places remains its normal color because the pressure blocks the blood vessels. This prevents blood from reaching and pooling in that area. Livor mortis can help a pathologist determine if a body was moved after death.

Wounds

Wounds help a pathologist determine how a person died or was injured. Wounds include needle-prick marks, scratches, bites, bullet holes, and stab wounds. When a person struggles with their attacker and tries to protect themselves, they may receive defense wounds. An absence of defense wounds could suggest that a person was taken by surprise or injured from a distance.

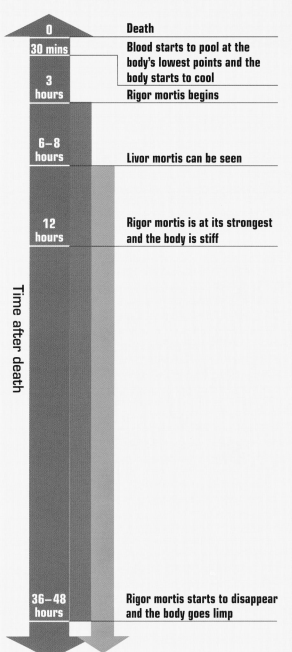

Timeline of death

Time after death

0	Death
30 mins	Blood starts to pool at the body's lowest points and the body starts to cool
3 hours	Rigor mortis begins
6–8 hours	Livor mortis can be seen
12 hours	Rigor mortis is at its strongest and the body is stiff
36–48 hours	Rigor mortis starts to disappear and the body goes limp

Internal Examinations

Internal examinations are carried out during **autopsies**. These examinations are vital for determining the cause and, possibly, time of death. Often the cause of death may look obvious, but an autopsy can reveal another story. Autopsies may also help in victim identification and tracing a victim's last steps.

Cause of Death

A victim recovered from a house fire did not necessarily die as a result of the fire. In these kinds of cases, the pathologist will always try to examine the victim's airways. If there are no traces of smoke or singeing in the airways, this shows the person died before the fire started. If they had been alive when the fire started, they would have inhaled lots of smoke, soot, and ash.

Similarly, a body dragged out of a river should have water in its lungs. If there is no water in the lungs, the person was dead before they entered the water.

A pathologist dissects and examines human tissue.

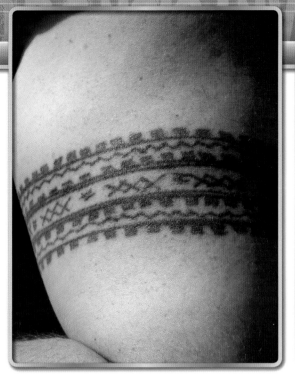

A tattoo is extremely helpful for victim identification.

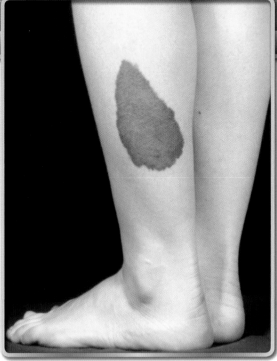

Birthmarks are also used to identify victims.

Identifying Victims

People can often be identified by their past medical history. Pathologists carefully look for identifying features such as signs of old bone fractures, past surgical procedures, and long-term organ damage. Tattoos and birthmarks can also help identify victims.

A Victim's Last Movements

Knowing a victim's movements before they died can help police in their investigations. A pathologist can examine a victim's stomach contents to help determine their last movements. If undigested breakfast cereal is found, this suggests that the victim died shortly after eating breakfast.

Stomach contents can also reveal where and with whom the victim was before they died. If Indian food is detected in a victim's stomach, police would search the victim's home for any sign of Indian food. If none was found, this could suggest that the victim had recently visited an Indian restaurant. Police could ask local Indian restaurants if and when they served the victim and who the victim was with.

Psychiatry and Psychology

The study of a person's mental state and their social behavior plays an important part in forensic investigations. Forensic psychiatrists assess the mental state of accused people to see if they are fit to go to trial or if they have a mental disorder. Forensic psychologists mainly work in offender profiling.

Offender Profiling

Profiling involves looking at all aspects of a crime to build up a personality profile of the offender. Usually, it is only possible to build up a detailed profile of repeat offenders, also called serial offenders.

Profiling has recently become more common due mainly to the work of John Douglas and Robert Ressler. These two men worked for the Federal Bureau of Investigation (FBI) Investigative Support Unit and interviewed hundreds of serial criminals. From these interviews, they built up a database of **motives**, crimes, and personalities associated with specific crimes.

John Douglas

Robert Ressler

> ### DID YOU KNOW?
> A person is not fit to go to trial if they have some types of mental illness, are drug affected, or have severe mental retardation, or major intellectual difficulties.

Details of an Offender Profile

Profiling is not an exact science and it does not identify an offender by name. Instead, it produces a highly detailed profile, which can be used to narrow down a list of suspects. It also helps police and prosecuting lawyers know how to deal with an offender to make them confess.

Some of the many details a profile can reveal about an offender are:

- age
- gender
- mental or behavioral disorders
- social problems, including any criminal record
- upbringing
- occupation
- marital status
- the car they might drive
- what area and type of place they are likely to live in
- with whom they are likely to live.

Profilers can often work out exactly how a crime was committed and the likely motive. In many cases, profiles developed by experts are very accurate and help cut down investigation time.

Ötzi the Iceman

Background

On September 19, 1991, some German hikers were trekking through the snow-covered Ötztal Alps, near the Austrian–Italian border. They came across a corpse, mostly buried in ice.

The Austrian authorities were called to remove and identify the body and to investigate the cause of death. The morgue in Innsbruck, where the corpse was taken, was in for a big surprise. This was not a recently dead person, but a corpse that was over 5,000 years old.

The Crime

Had a crime been committed? This was one of the major questions the investigators wanted to answer. Did Ötzi, also known as the Iceman, die of natural causes, in battle, or was he murdered? Using many forensic techniques, scientists from around the world revealed how Ötzi died and also how, where, and when he lived.

Ötzi is moved from where he was found in the Ötztal Alps, near the Austrian–Italian border.

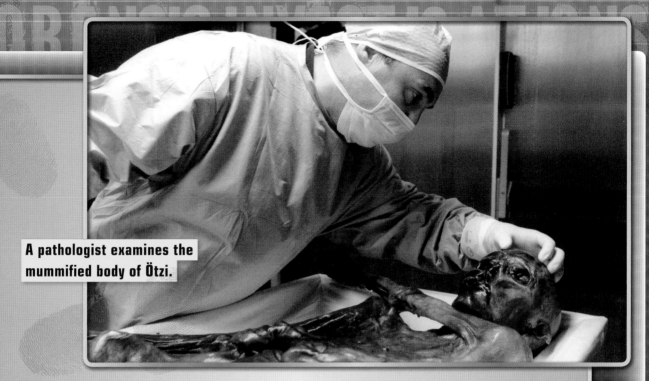

A pathologist examines the mummified body of Ötzi.

The Evidence

The ice had mummified Ötzi's body and his DNA, as well as parts of his clothing and tools, and traces of plant material. Below is just a small sample of what the evidence revealed.

• Examination of Ötzi's bones and teeth showed that he was a male aged about 45 years old and was 5-foot-5 (1.65m) tall. His skull showed signs of damage, indicating a major blow to the head. Some experts believe this blow caused Ötzi's death.

• X rays and scans revealed that Ötzi had an arrowhead lodged in one shoulder. Many experts believe that this injury caused Ötzi to bleed to death. Ötzi also had bruises and cuts on his hands, wrists, and chest, indicating a fight.

• DNA was recovered from blood found on Ötzi's clothes and tools. The DNA came from Ötzi and four other people, suggesting that a fight or battle had taken place.

Over the past 20 years, investigations have revealed that Ötzi died sometime between 3350 BCE and 3300 BCE. He lived his entire life within 31 miles (50km) of where he was found and he was most likely a shepherd.

Investigating the Investigators

Most forensic investigators are police members with a science, engineering, or other relevant university degree. Outside experts are also involved. The following investigators are just some of the experts involved in investigations that involve biological evidence and offender profiling.

Forensic Anthropologists

Forensic anthropologists study human physical development. They are called on to help identify victims or their cause of death by studying skeletal remains. They often work closely with forensic dentists.

Forensic Pathologists

Forensic pathologists are medical doctors who specialize in carrying out autopsies. Their main role is to determine how, when, and where a person died, but they also examine wounds on surviving victims. Pathologists often examine bloodstain patterns at the crime scene.

Forensic Biologists

Forensic biologists are specialists who interpret bloodstain patterns, carry out blood typing, and analyze DNA.

Psychiatrists

Psychiatrists are medical doctors who specialize in mental illnesses and mental disorders. Forensic psychiatrists determine if an accused's mental state led to them committing the crime, if the accused is mentally fit to stand trial, and the best way to treat a mentally ill offender. Some psychiatrists also carry out offender profiling.

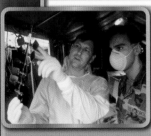

Odontologists

Odontologists are dentists who study the structure, development, and any abnormalities of the teeth. These dentists are often used in forensic investigations, especially in bite mark examinations and to help identify bodies.

Psychologists

Forensic psychologists are not medical doctors and cannot prescribe medicines. They mainly work on offender profiling and may also be involved in the treatment of criminals with mental problems.

Glossary

ante-mortem	before death
autopsies	the examination of bodies to determine the time and cause of death
clotting factors	substances in the blood that help stop blood flow
database	computer systems that hold data, such as fingerprints, that can be accessed by different people
enzyme	protein found in the body that can cut DNA and other proteins
forensic pathologists	medical doctors who specialize in carrying out autopsies
genetic information	information relating to genes, DNA, and inherited characteristics
hair sheaths	thin layers of cells that surround the hair roots
incident	violent, dangerous, or criminal event
ligaments	flexible tissue that connects two bones together
livor mortis	the natural settling of blood in the body after death, also called post-mortem lividity
mortuary	the place where autopsies are carried out or bodies are stored
motives	reasons for doing things
odontologist	dentist who studies the structure, development, and any abnormalities of the teeth
pores	tiny openings in a surface
post-mortem	after death
rigor mortis	the stiffening of the body shortly after death

Index